I0166818

William L. Merry

The Nicaragua Canal

The gateway between the oceans

William L. Merry

The Nicaragua Canal
The gateway between the oceans

ISBN/EAN: 9783337319304

Printed in Europe, USA, Canada, Australia, Japan

Cover: Foto ©Andreas Hilbeck / pixelio.de

More available books at **www.hansebooks.com**

THE
NICARAGUA CANAL

THE GATEWAY BETWEEN THE OCEANS

Published by Authority of

THE CHAMBER OF COMMERCE OF SAN FRANCISCO
THE BOARD OF TRADE OF SAN FRANCISCO
THE CHAMBER OF COMMERCE OF PORTLAND, OREGON
THE CHAMBER OF COMMERCE OF SAN DIEGO

WILLIAM L. MERRY

The Commercial Organizations Which Have United in This Publication For
the Public Interest, Respectfully Request That All Who Desire
to Increase the Prestige and Commerce of Our Country
and the Prosperity of the Pacific Coast,
Will Aid in Giving It as Wide a
Circulation as Possible.

SAN FRANCISCO, CALIFORNIA

1895

PRESS OF COMMERCIAL PUB. CO., 34 CALIFORNIA ST.

Contents.

"The landmark to the double tide
That purpling rolls on either side,
As if their waters chafed to meet
Yet pause and crouch beneath her feet."

—*Byron,* "*The Siege of Corinth.*"

Technical Details.

Total Distance from Ocean to Ocean	169.4 miles
Canal in Excavation	*26.8 "
Lengths of Basins	21.6 "
River San Juan	64.5 "
Lake Nicaragua	56.5 "
Free Navigation in Lake, River and Basins	142.6 "
Elevation of Summit Level of Canal above Sea Level	110 feet
Length of Summit Level	153.2 miles
Number of Locks	6
Greatest Lift of Lock	45 feet
Dimensions of Locks	650 feet long, 80 feet wide
Depth of Canal	30 feet
Least Width at Bottom	100 "
Time Transit From Ocean to Ocean	28 hours
Length of Lake Nicaragua	110 miles
Average Width	40 "
Surface Area	about 2,600 square miles
Area of Watershed of Lake	" 8,000 " "

*A remarkable fact.

Dedication.

TO THE PIONEER MERCHANTS OF THE PACIFIC COAST,

Who, over trackless plains, around the Cape of Storms, across the Isthmus of Panama,
or through beautiful Nicaragua,
Forced their Way to and Laid the Foundation of our Pacific Empire,
This Book,
Issued by the Commercial Organizations by Them Established,
Is Respectfully Dedicated.

WILLIAM L. MERRY.

General U. S. Grant, North American Review.
February, 1881.

" In accordance with the early and later policy of the Government ; in obedience to the often expressed will of the American people ; with a due regard to our national dignity and power ; with a watchful care for the safety and prosperity of our interests and industries on this Continent ; and with a determination to guard against even the first approach of rival powers, whether friendly or hostile, on these shores, *I commend an American Canal on American soil to the American people*, and congratulate myself on the fact that the most careful explorations have been started, and that the route standing in this attitude before the world, is the one which commends itself as a *judicious, economical* and *prosperous* work ."

Report of the Commission appointed by the President of the United States in 1872 "to Examine Into, Make Suggestions and Report Upon the Subject of Inter-Oceanic Ship Canal Communication."

WASHINGTON CITY, February 7th, 1876.

To the President of the United States:

The Commission appointed by you to consider the subject of communication by canal, between the waters of the Atlantic and Pacific Oceans, across, over, or near the isthmus connecting North and South America, have the honor, after a long, careful, and minute study of the several surveys of the various routes across the continent, unanimously to report:

That the route known as the " *Nicaragua Route* " beginning on the Atlantic side at or near Greytown, running by canal to the San Juan River * * * from thence across the lake and through the valleys of the Rio del Medio and the Rio Grande to what is known as the Port of Brito, on the Pacific Coast, possesses, both for the construction and maintenance of a canal, greater advantages and offers fewer difficulties from engineering, commercial and economic points of view than any of the other routes shown to be practicable by surveys sufficiently in detail to enable a judgment to be formed of their relative merits, as will be briefly presented in the appended memorandum. We have the honor to be, with high respect,

Your obedient servants,

DANIEL AMMEN, U. S. N.,
Commodore and Chief of Bureau of Navigation.

ANDREW A. HUMPHREYS,
Brigadier-General, Chief of Engineers, U. S. A., etc.

C. P. PATTERSON,
Superintendent U. S. Coast Survey.

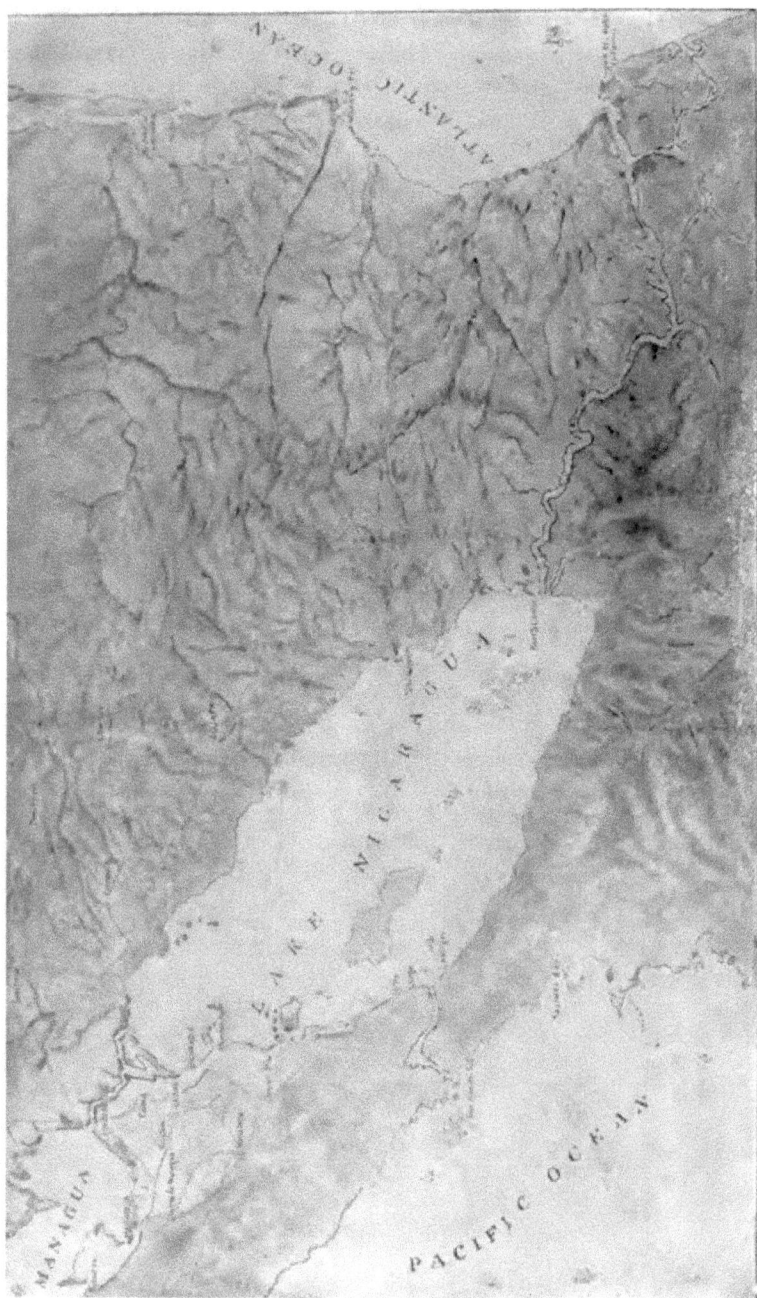

MAP OF THE MARITIME CANAL OF NICARAGUA.

THE NICARAGUA CANAL.

Its Commercial Necessity.

On the Pacific Coast of the United States the commercial necessity for the prompt construction of the Nicaragua Canal is so obvious that it finds no opponents worthy of consideration. The Southern States are almost equally interested, and two great Canal Conventions have been held there to promote it. The Eastern seaboard States are also ardent advocates of the Canal, and what indifference to the beneficent enterprise exists today, is found in the Middle West, where its immediate benefits are not so evident to the casual observer, although easily demonstrated upon examination. It is a notable fact however, that the citizens of the great interior city of Chicago, renowned for her enterprise and commercial activity, are among the most ardent advocates of the Canal, and are fully cognizant of its advantage to them, when, by means of a navigable water-way to the Gulf, to be completed in 1896, they shall have an outlet to the Ocean very near to the Gateway of the Pacific.

The Pacific Coast of the United States is isolated from our Eastern and from European markets by a continent over three thousand miles wide, with two mountain ranges over which the locomotive must climb, with ponderous loads, at heavy cost, and by a sea voyage of nearly 15,000 miles, around Cape Horn. It suffers from commercial isolation, modified, however, in recent years by the construction of five overland railways and by the opening of Isthmus routes at Panama and Tehuantepec, while Guatemala and Costa Rica are also striving to obtain outlets on the Atlantic Coast. The railways crossing the continental mountain chains to the Atlantic, are powerless for the provision of cheap transportation for the bulky products of our soil, although very valuable for rapid transportation, with which the Canal can not interfere to an extent which will offset the benefit they will receive from it. For many years to come we must look to our Eastern sea coast and to the continent of Europe for our principal markets. Great changes are being inaugurated in Eastern Asia which may ultimately open for us new markets there, but for a long future, our main reliance will be upon Atlantic markets, while our geographical position gives us advantages in Eastern Asiatic markets, when conditions shall enable us to develop them more rapidly. Under the present conditions Asiatic merchandise which would naturally be distributed from Pacific Seaports is, by the railroad policy of competition with the Suez Canal diverted to Eastern cities, San Francisco having in this respect been seriously discriminated against. The Canal will remedy this. When completed, the Suez Canal will no longer be a factor to the detriment of our Asiatic import trade. The Atlantic Coast will be supplied through the Nicaragua Canal, steamships calling at San Francisco and San Diego en route to the Atlantic, for the reason that the "*great circle*" or shortest ocean route from Eastern Asiatic seaports, passes within 180 miles of San Francisco and 130 miles of San Diego! As the diversion from the great circle, when steering for Pacific Ports, would be made at about the 180th degree Meridian, the loss in distance created thereby would be approximately one half of the above distance, in fact not appreciable. When thus calling at our ports, these Atlantic bound steamships loaded at Asiatic ports, would partly *duplicate their earnings* by discharging a portion of their cargo here and replacing it with Pacific **Coast** products for Atlantic ports, while coaling. *Thus the tide of Asiatic commerce to the Atlantic would enter our Pacific Ports,* while as far Eastward as the Mississippi River, our railways will be able to distribute Asiatic merchandise in competition with Gulf and Atlantic ports, with the advantage of position in our favor. To demonstrate what I have here asserted, let the reader draw a flexible string tightly, on a large globe, between Yokohama and the Pacific terminus of the Nicaragua Canal, and the argument will be made plain. All Asiatic commerce to the Pacific Coast, by steam, and in less degree by sail, must pass near Japan, and thus the argument applies to it as an entirety. This branch of the subject is worthy of more time than can at present be given it, but no one who has investigated it, contests the necessary results herein set forth.

I pass on to our commerce with the Atlantic, first Eastward, for the reason that, upon the profitable marketing of the products of our soil and industry, depends more largely than any one factor, the prosperity of our Pacific Coast. For years to come our people will be principally producers. Manufacturing except for local purposes, is generally done at a disadvantage with competing Eastern and European points. Coal, wages and labor are all higher here than there, and the manufacturer cannot expect to succeed in the export trade unless he can compete in price and quality ; to expect more than a preference at the same price, is more than can be justly asked and more than will be generally accorded by buyers. I do not wish to be understood as underrating the importance of developing Pacific Coast manufactures ; indeed, no effort should be spared to encourage them, as any community which depends upon production alone is at a great disadvantage, and we should, by every means, develop the local pride which prefers a home manufactured article, a point wherein our people have been and are remiss to their detriment.

It is in the elimination of about 10,000 miles on our cheap water route for the products of the Pacific Coast that the Nicaragua Canal will the most benefit us. Ten thousand miles ! Equal to twice across the Pacific Ocean, and nearly half the circumference of the globe ! Hereafter I shall prove how much cheaper than any other communication is freight carried by water, especially upon Ocean routes. The evidences of this are all around us and are universally admitted. I shall particularize in some of the principal productive industries, but the limits of this paper will not permit the consideration of all the benefits to our producers to be secured by a short water route to the Atlantic.

Our lumber trade has for years been in a very unsatisfactory condition. It is an industry with very heavy investments, and enormous possibilities, and it has not been remunerative by reason of our isolation from the great markets of the World. The output has been greatly restricted by agreement, and even with this precaution there has generally been no profit in the industry. Our export is limited to an occasional cargo for Australia, South Africa, South America, with invoices to Mexico and Central America. Europe and our Eastern seaboard is denuded of timber, while the demand on the Southern and Middle Western States has of late years been so heavy that those sections are being rapidly stripped of timber. On the Pacific Coast, there is an

NOTE—Steamships en route from Yokohama to the Atlantic, via Canal will lose only 91 knots by calling at San Francisco, and from Hongkong only 20 knots. The reader's attention is

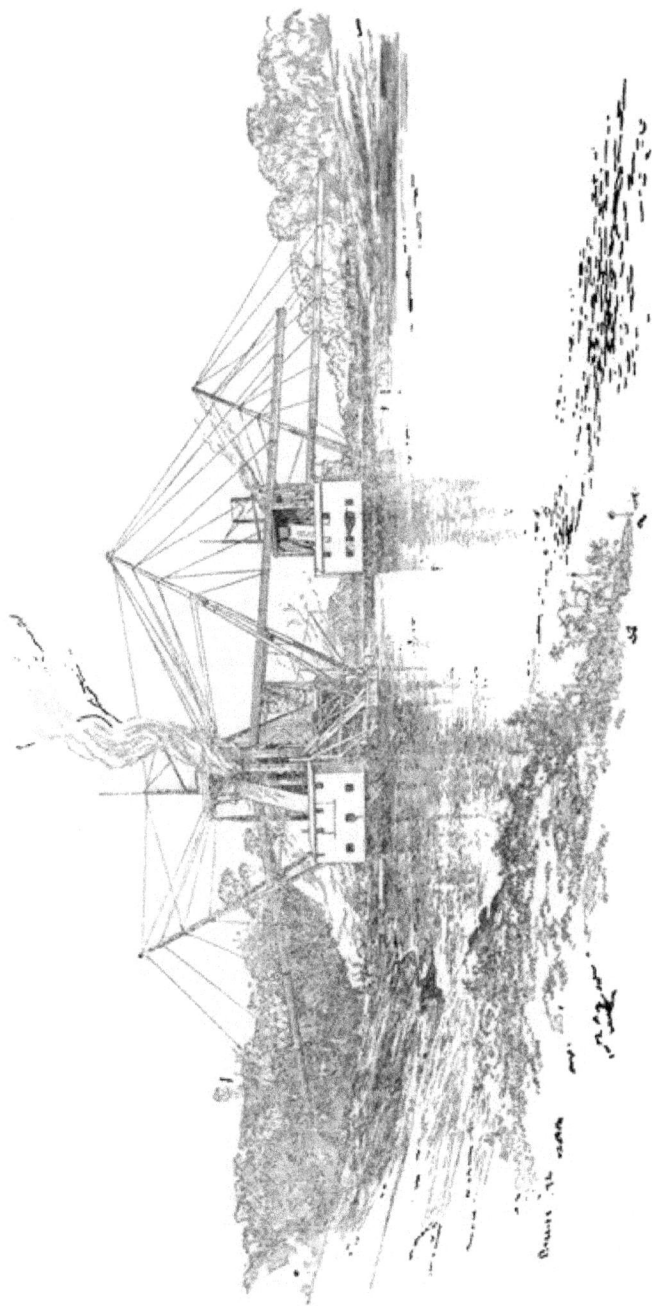

DREDGES AT WORK ON CANAL NEAR ATLANTIC TERMINUS.

enormous supply, the undisturbed growth of ages, and the completion of the Canal
will inaugurate a tremendous development of this trade. It will enhance values of
timber lands far more than the entire cost of the Canal, and employ a great amount of
shipping, a large part of which will be documented under the American flag, thus
creating activity in American shipyards and iron industries. The demand for our
redwood and Oregon pine will exceed all anticipations as they have no equals for
special purposes, in the world's supply of lumber. These facts are so thoroughly understood by our lumber merchants that they have for years been ardent supporters of the
Nicaragua Canal.

Our wheat industry is in a lamentable condition, and generally unremunerative for
export. Indeed, it has, so far as export is concerned, been a gamble with the forces of
nature. A five months voyage around the Cape has made it impossible to do more
than hope for a successful shipment, since no man can correctly estimate the world's
supply during the ensuing season, months ahead, and it is a noticeable fact that all
the heaviest San Francisco wheat deals have been financial failures.

India through the Suez Canal, Russia near by, and Argentine within twenty-five
days of European markets, control the trade against us, both in time and distance ; they
" *have the call*" and we come in at the tail end ! Consider the magic change of an
open canal ! New York in eighteen days, and Europe in twenty-five days, easy steam-
ing, will place our wheat dealers in fair competition with all the world ! It will no
longer be necessary to charter and load an entire ship. Cargo steamers will carry
invoices direct from producers if they wish and the gambling element in our present
wheat shipments will be eliminated. A quick delivery will make it practically a cash
trade, on a safe basis of small profits and a large volume of business, done mostly by
steamers, bringing European passengers and merchandise westward. The saving on
wheat freights would have already furnished money enough to build the Canal, although
of recent years freights via the Cape have often been low, but they can never be low
enough by that 15,000 mile route to offset the disadvantages alluded to.

Our fruit industry will receive a great impetus when the Canal is open to it. In
the transportation of fresh fruit *time* is an important factor, and by rail freights must
always be comparatively high. It is encouraging that improved methods tend to reduce
the cost of transportation, and in this industry railways can better compete with the
Canal than in the others so far named, for the demand is largely in the interior of the
Continent, and to such points as a comparatively high freight can be paid, leaving a
profit to the producer.

But the modern refrigerator, as applied to steamships, has solved the question of
cheap transportation of perishable products by sea. Thousand of tons of fresh beef,
mutton, etc., are now always en route from Australia and New Zealand to Europe in
refrigerator steamships. Meat products require a temperature of 22° to 26° Farh. for
safe keeping, while fruits require 36° to 38° Farh. for preservation ; a dry
atmosphere being needed in both cases. Partial cargoes of fresh fruit are now being
successfully shipped from Cape Colony to Europe, across the Equator, under conditions
much less favorable than they would be via the Nicaragua Canal.

When our horticulturists have the markets of Northern Europe open to them at a
low cost, in 25 days, by refrigerator steamers, the fear of an overproduction may be
safely dismissed. Our fruits, large and small, and our vegetables are luxuries in North-

ern Europe, with a market limited only by the cost to consumers. Our production is so rapidly increasing that by the time the Canal can be opened it will be needed. That this is fully appreciated is proven by the ardent support given the Canal by all our horticulturists, the energetic people of Southern California being especially pronounced in this demand for a short waterway to the Atlantic.

The trade with Japan in raw cotton is comparatively new and rapidly increasing, as the manufacture of cotton fabrics in that Empire is developing immensely. Japan can purchase a short staple cotton in India, but must place her main dependence upon the American staple. This will go to her through the Canal, furnishing return cargoes to steamships carrying Asiatic goods to our Gulf Ports. This trade has an immense future, for it means the supply of 47,000,000 people with cheap clothing and other cotton fabrics.

In no part of the world are *coal and iron* found in greater proximity than in Alabama, and that section of the Union can supply the Pacific Coast and Pacific Islands with great facility through the Canal. This will be a great benefit to us, until these industries can be developed here. All the steam coal needed on the Canal and at the Naval Station on Lake Nicaragua can be thus supplied with an excellent article at very low prices, towed there in barges from Mobile.

The fisheries of the Northwest Pacific Coast and Islands have a great future. The discoveries of fishing banks already made by the United States steamship "*Albatross*" prove this assertion and the exploration has only been started. Although overland railways will largely deal with this industry, supplying the interior of the Continent by the service of refrigerator cars, the Canal will offer a cheap highway for fishing vessels to and from the Atlantic coasts, carrying homeward their own catch, using San Francisco or other Pacific Coast ports as points of departure for the homeward voyage

The Pacific Coast needs *a desirable immigration*. This the railways have been unable to develop; it has always cost too much to get here, and Eastern localities have consequently received general preference. While our people have a conviction that our immigration laws are much too lax and that a bad citizen in Europe makes a worse citizen here, the fact remains that the Canal will be largely used by European and Atlantic Coast immigrants who will settle up our idle lands, open our mines and create new industries ; largely a consuming class. And our position warrants us in expecting that we shall receive the best class of settlers, because it will still cost more to get here from Europe than the Atlantic seaboard. Our lands will gradually be subdivided and we shall no longer see the abnormal spectacle of a magnificent valley like that of the Sacramento decreasing in population, and in small land holdings. The Canal will create an urgent demand for American built shipping and for seamen to man it. It is in fact, admitted that the tonnage via Canal in the American coastwise trade will be entirely inadequate to meet the demand, when the Canal is open and until it can be constructed in our shipyards. While steamships will gradually obtain preference, the use of sailing ships via Nicaragua Canal, unlike the Suez Canal, is entirely practicable. This maritime development will make San Francisco a great seaport and restore to it the position it occupied in its early history, but on a greatly enlarged scale. The same remark applies to other Pacific Coast ports in a degree corresponding with the facilities they offer and the support they receive from their tributary territory.

LAKE NICARAGUA, OMETEPE ISLAND IN THE DISTANCE.

I might go on with illustrations but other branches of the subject demand consideration, and they are not needed by the intelligent merchant. It would indeed be a difficult, if not an impossible task, to predict *all* the changes which the construction of the canal will inaugurate. It needs the prescience of a statesman; the commercial acumen of a merchant, and the technical skill of a navigator, to correctly estimate the effect of eliminating a navigation of 10,000 miles for all the maritime nations of the World. Such a stupendous change in the geography of the globe must create radical changes, but of this we may rest assured; they will be changes for the advantage of human progress, for commerce recognizes no nationality, and, more than any other agency, tends to unite the human race in the great brotherhood of mutual interest. For us, the Canal means the reverse of the Pioneer condition of commercial isolation. Already partly destroyed by other agencies, we are halting in the march of progress; an arrested development which will be terminated by the completion of the Nicaragua Canal. The Canal means development and progress, so far as can now be judged, without injury to any existing interest on the Pacific Coast.

The tolls which commerce can afford to pay for the use of the Canal have been a proper question of inquiry. Utilizing the locks by electric lights at night, the Canal can pass 20,240,000 tons annually, which can be doubled by duplicating the locks. The Suez Canal has passed over 9,000,000 tons annually, producing a revenue of 15 @ 19 per cent. In the estimate of tonnage that will use the Nicaragua Canal, the coastwise commerce of the United States must always prove an important and increasing factor. Already an immense commerce, it has no practical limit until the Great Republic shall have been closely populated. No other inter-oceanic canal can compete for this immense carrying trade, while Great Britain will make use of both Nicaragua and Suez Canals for her colonial trade.

A careful estimate of the tonnage within the radius of attraction by the Canal in 1891, made it 8,159,150 tons, but the annual increase is a matter of opinion, and has therefore been placed at the low estimate of 6½ per cent. approximately for the intervening period until completion, in five years. In this connection I may state that, while the time allowed for construction has been fixed at five years, it may be largely reduced by the use of electric lighting, possibly to three years from the active inauguration of work, the estimate made having been based on a ten hours per day labor. It is a noticeable fact that in 1894, of the steamships passing through the Suez Canal, 95 per cent. continued their passage at night by use of the electric lights, navigating in safety; a more difficult problem than the use of electric lights for construction work. We have assurances of 8,730,000 tons for the Nicaragua Canal by the time it can be completed; possibly this is an under estimate. This, at $1.85 per ton, (the charge now made at Suez) will produce $16,150,500 annual revenue. The cost of maintenance and improvements may be safely estimated $1,500,000 annually, leaving $14,-650,500 net revenue, on a cost which should not exceed $100,000,000 and which may not be over $80,000,000, if built by the aid of the Government credit. Like the Suez Canal, it will be one of the best paying properties in the World.

The Canal will make large earnings also on through passengers, not only on European immigrants westward, but on tourists. The route will be a romantic one, through a delightful trade wind climate. There is no finer scenery in the world; no more attractive combination of land and water, than the Nicaragua Lakes and the River San

Juan, both well remembered by many old Californians. Travellers will always desire to pass through the Canal at least once, and, as on a low rate speed, the trip from San Francisco to New York or return can be made in fifteen days, it will attract great travel.

The American continent extending into the Southern Ocean over 21 degrees of latitude more than Africa, the navigation around Cape Horn is over 2594 miles longer than around the Cape of Good Hope and much more dangerous. The distances saved by the canal at Nicaragua are generally much greater than at Suez, a fact which will tend to augment its revenue. The Suez Canal diverted an already established commerce without much prospect of additional development, while the Nicaragua Canal will develop a commerce already of large volume, but the tributary nations are largely in their infancy of development, and with a certainty of enormous increase in wealth, population and commerce.

There is another source of revenue not heretofore alluded to in public discussion of the subject, although of great importance. I refer to the local commerce of Nicaragua. The Nicaragua Canal, besides being a great inter-oceanic highway, is *an internal channel of communication and commerce*, for a Country with great resources, and in this respect is unique: Suez passes through a desert. Immediately that the Canal is open the magnificent region surrounding the Nicaragua Lakes will teem with a new life and a development of its great resources. It is one of the most productive Countries on the globe, producing all the tropical and semi-tropical products, largely timbered with cabinet hard woods, rich in mines of gold and silver, and blessed with a splendid climate, as will hereafter be proven. I do not hazard much in the assertion that, within ten years after the opening of the Canal, this local traffic will produce enough revenue to pay all operating expenses, and the nation that builds the Canal will have the greatest part of this trade.

The diversion of commerce from Pacific Coast ports by means of the Canal has been occasionally stated as against its utility, but on careful examination there will be found no reason to apprehend this to any extent. As before stated, so far from Asiatic commerce being diverted, it will enter our portals, and we shall have the advantage of location in distribution eastward overland, until it meets the same class of merchandise coming up the Mississippi Valley, from the Canal. Australian Commerce to Europe and our Atlantic Coast will certainly go via Canal, but this will work no injury to us, for now it goes either via Suez Canal or Cape of Good hope, while our location should enable us to develope a large direct trade with Australasia. Hawaiian commerce should, under natural conditions always be controlled by American Pacific Ports, as the interchange of products is natural and mutually beneficial. Occasional cargoes will go from the Hawaiian Islands through the Canal, to Atlantic Ports, but this is now the case via Cape Horn, several sugar cargoes going that way this season. But this will be abnormal under any condition which can now be foreseen.

The commerce of Central America, except in regard to such demand as we have for the products of that section, is constantly striving for an Atlantic outlet. The Tehuantepec Railway the Guatemala Northern Railway to Livingston, and the Costa Rica Railway to Port Limon, (both on the Atlantic) and the Panama Railway, all facilitate the movement of Central American products to the Atlantic. Under no circumstances can we expect to attract this European and Atlantic Coast demand for Central American products to our Pacific Coasts ports; they can be transported cheaper by the routes named at this time and cheaper still through the Canal.

But the Canal will rapidly develop the resources and increase the population of all Central America, Nicaragua taking precedence in this particular as it is to be the first scene of a new activity. With these improved conditions will come an increase of commerce with United States Pacific Ports, and our Pacific Coast railway systems will find it to their advantage to distribute Eastward, the products of Central America in competition with Gulf Ports distributing Northward, or Atlantic Coast Ports Westward. The advantage of location will be with us, and we shall have to pay no Canal toll, while the increasing wealth and population of Central America will take from us in vastly

MARKET SCENE AT GRANADA CITY, ON LAKE NICARAGUA.

increased quantity the products we are now sending there ; flour, canned fruits and meats, California wines, and many other articles now being shipped there by every steamer. And Central American products will be marketed here in greater quantity as a merchandise basis of exchange. A diversion of commerce from our Pacific Coast Ports has never been mentioned in any other connection. But I may state here, that it is an erroneous view of the Canal to consider it solely for our benefit, and such a position, besides being false in fact, would defeat its construction. In a general way I may state that commercially, the Canal will benefit first, the Pacific Coast of North

FORT CASTILLO AND VILLAGE, LOOKING UP RIVER SAN JUAN.

Brown 71

America ; second, the Gulf Coast of the United States ; third, the East Coast of the United States ; fourth, the Valley of the Mississippi and the great middle West of the United States ; fifth, the West Coast of South America and the Pacific Islands. Other parts of the World would be benefited also, in less degree, and the commerce of all maritime nations will be greatly facilitated thereby. Its advantages, otherwise than commercial I shall illustrate hereafter.

To the shipping merchant, seaman and stevedore the advantages of carrying merchandise without " *breaking bulk* " are very well known. It is the rough handling of packages in transshipment, and their exposure to a tropical, often also to a moisture laden climate, that has proven the principal deterrent to the popular use of the Isthmus transits for freight. The additional expense is also to be considered, but it is doubtful if the prior consideration is not the most important. The Canal will make this unnecessary, and the merchandise placed on board will remain untouched until delivery at destination. Wheat and other grains can be shipped in bulk as is now done on the Atlantic, thus saving the onerous expense of sacking, which must be borne by the producer, amounting to about one dollar per ton. It may be safely asserted that approximately ninety per cent. of claims for damage on freight are due to handling and ten per cent. to bad stowage and sea-damage, if total losses be excluded.

It is no small honor to the Chamber of Commerce and to the Board of Trade of San Francisco that these two organizations are the pioneer promoters of the Nicaragua Canal, from a commercial stand point. Illustrious statesmen have pointed out its advantages to our Country, and military experts have demonstrated its necessity to the national safety of the Great Republic, but our merchants have been the first to present it to the commercial world as the great project of the age. In 1880 I was daily requested to explain wherein the Canal would benefit us ; in 1895 I am asked on all sides what are the prospects for its completion and it is universally recognized as worthy of the support of all who wish well to the Pacific Coast, and of all patriotic Americans who desire to see their country holding its place and fulfilling its destiny among the great nations of the earth.

THE NICARAGUA CANAL.

Description and History.

The Republic of Nicaragua lies between Honduras and Salvador on the north and Costa Rica on the south. It has a coast line of 250 miles on the Atlantic and 185 miles on the Pacific Ocean. From ocean to ocean it is 200 miles wide on its northern boundary and 120 miles wide on its southern boundary. It extends from latitude 10° to 15° north. Its area is 49,000 square miles, (about three times the area of Switzerland) and its estimated population is 450,000 souls. The eastern coast was first sighted by Columbus in 1503. It was first visited and explored by the Spanish military adventurer, Gil Gonzales Davila in 1522. In 1821 the five Central American Republics, including Nicaragua, became independent of Spain, and formed a confederacy which was dissolved in 1839, since which they have been independent. The Republic derives its name from *Nicarao* a native chief found on the shores of the great lake by the Spanish discoverer, who called the lake *Nicarao-agua*, from which came the abbreviation Nicaragua.

From Cape Horn to the Arctic Ocean a continuous mountain chain rears its peaks between the oceans, under various names, but always the same longest of all mountain systems in the world, But in Nicaragua occurs a freak of nature. The mountain range is broken and decreased in elevation. Two great lakes Nicaragua and Managua, depress the continental back bone and furnish the lowest level between the Atlantic and Pacific Oceans, from Cape Horn to the Arctic Ocean ; 152 6-12 feet above mean sea level. The next lowest is at Panama 295 feet, and Tehuantepec has an elevation of 855 feet. Lake Nicaragua is 110 miles long and 40 miles wide. Standing on its western shore, its waves beat at the traveller's feet with the cadence of an ocean surf and the opposite shore is out of sight, It is from 12 to 240 feet deep and free from hidden dangers, except that its waters are infested with sharks, having probably come from the Carribbean sea and gradually became habituated to the new environment, as in the case of the sharks in the lakes of the Feejee Islands.

Lake Managua is thirty miles long and fifteen wide, of an irregular shape and twenty-four feet higher than Lake Nicaragua. It is proposed to unite these two lakes by a canal with one lock to overcome the difference in elevation. This work is included in the Canal Company's contract with the Government. These two great lakes and the consequent low summit level between the oceans, give to Nicaragua an especially fine climate—it may be called a *marine tropical climate*. The trade winds from the Atlantic blow, with rare exceptions, across the republic, minimizing malarial influences and lowering the thermometer, so that at night one needs a blanket to sleep comfortably in the vicinity of the lakes.

Among the many advantages possessed by this favored land, there is one which far exceeds in value her resources of mine, field and forest. Standing midway between the northern and southern extremities of the continents, the barrier there presented to direct communication between the two great oceans, and the countries bordering upon them is, usbefore stated, the lowest that exists anywhere on the American Continent. The import of this great fact to the commercial world remains to be considered. We merely remark that Nicaragua is *on the highway of the world's future commerce*, and in a military point of view far exceeds Gibraltar in importance. It is, in fact, *the key between the Atlantic and the Pacific — the path of empire is through its gateway for the nation that holds the key!*

The Republic is divided into thirteen Departments, each governed by a Prefect. Otherwise the form of government is similar to that of the United States; there is entire liberty of religious belief and much attention is paid to public education. There are several small cities in the Republic; *Leon* with 30,000 inhabitants; *Granada* with 15,000; *Chinandega* with 12,000; *Managua*, the capital city, with 10,000; *Masaya* with 8,000; *Rivas*, four miles from the Canal, Western Division, with 7,000; *Matagalpa*, (in the famous coffee district) with 4,000; and *La Libertad* with 4,000. Besides these there are several smaller seaport towns; *Corinto*, lately the scene of British military occupation and evacuation; *Brito* and *San Juan del Sur* on the Pacific, and *San Juan del Norte* and *Bluefields* on the Atlantic, as well as others of minor importance. There are few good roads in the country, transportation being slow and expensive, except by water and on the two excellent railways, which are well managed, as well as owned, by the Government. The Republic was primarily settled on the Pacific Coast, but lately the industry of banana and cocoanut growing has so increased on the so-called Mosquito Coast, that two regular lines of weekly steamers run to New Orleans and twice a month to Colon, and the Eastern coast is being rapidly settled. Between the Atlantic and Lake Nicaragua there are rich mineral districts with gold and silver mines which have been worked for many years, two of them being owned in London. This section of the Republic is also largely devoted to cattle raising, and the Republic produces all the products of a tropical and semi-tropical climate.

The availability of the Nicaragua route for an inter-oceanic highway was indicated as early as 1550 by the Spanish explorer, Antonio Galvao. Since 1825 the subject has been repeatedly presented to the Governments of Nicaragua and the United States. In 1844 Don Francisco Castellan, a citizen of Nicaragua, visited France, and the project was by him called to the attention of Louis Napoleon, who published a pamphlet on the subject, but no active efforts followed. In 1849 Cornelius Vanderbilt and associates obtained a concession for a ship canal, and a remarkably correct survey was made for them by Colonel Childs of Philadelphia, which was pronounced feasible by United States Government and English engineers.

In 1852 a series of explorations were commenced, covering the whole isthmus, partly on private account, but mostly under instructions of the United States Government. In 1872–73 complete surveys of Nicaragua and Panama routes were made by Commander Lull, United States Navy, with Mr. A. G. Menocal as the Chief Engineer. The result of their instrumental surveys was the condemnation of the Panama route and the official approval of the Nicaragua route for a lock canal, using the great lake as its summit level. Their surveys demonstrated the possibility of a lock canal at Panama with fourteen feet more elevation than at Nicaragua, and at greater cost. It entirely condemned the Panama route for a sea level canal, as afterwards attempted by the French. General Grant, himself a civil engineer of no mean pretensions, wrote in the North American Review of February, 1881, that if practicable at all, the Panama Canal would cost over $400,000,000. He is also on record as asserting that every dollar put into the Panama Canal would be lost to the investors.

DREDGES AT WORK—LAND VIEW. EMBANKMENT OF CANAL AND CONSTRUCTION RAILWAY TRAIN.

In May 1879 Lesseps called together the International Canal Congress at Paris for the assumed purpose of consultation as to the route to be adopted. The United States Government appointed Rear Admiral Daniel Ammen, United States Navy, and Mr. A. G. Menocal, C. E. as our delegates. It appearing that the Congress was controlled in the interest of parties who had acquired a concession for the Panama route, and that a fair discussion and vote was not wanted, our delegates declined to vote. It subsequently appeared that a French syndicate, including Count de Lesseps and Gustave Blanchet, C. E. had made a prior application to the Nicaragua Government for a concession, and failing there, had taken up the Wyse-Turr concession from the Columbian Government for a canal at Panama, subject to the prior rights of the Panama Railroad Company, and these concessionaires had offered Lesseps' inducements to join them in promoting the enterprise.

The failure of Lesseps' application to the Nicaragua Government recalls an interesting incident. At that time *Fernando Guzman* was President of Nicaragua. Educated in the United States and France, he was a wise and patriotic statesman. The French Canal bill was introduced simultaneously in the Chamber of Deputies and Senate. It passed the former, and was lost by one vote in the latter A motion to reconsider was made and the Senate adjourned. President Guzman, when informed of the result, sent for the Senator who moved for reconsideration and, while disclaiming any right to interfere with the action of the Senate, informed him that, unless he was confident of enough votes to pass the bill over the veto, it would be time wasted. The Senator expressed suprise and asked for a reason, as he deemed the Canal a great benefit to Nicaragua. Guzman answered by asking him " if he remembered the French military occupation of Mexico and their attempt to destroy the Republic there," remarking also that, if they built the Canal they would ultimately control the country, and treat Nicaragua as they had treated Mexico ; that the Americans " want the Canal and will not destroy our Government " and if the French did not build it, the American people or Government would. This failure of the French to obtain a Canal concession from Nicaragua was sedulously concealed, while the Panama Canal was being floated, and this incident answers the oft repeated inquiry why did not Lesseps go to Nicaragua if it is so much the best route for a ship canal ?

In 1880 a " Provisional Canal Society" was formed at New York including Gen. Grant, Gen. McLellan, Admiral Ammen, Frederick Billings and others. In May 1880 the Society obtained a Canal concession from the Nicaraguan Government and in Dec. 1881 a bill was introduced by Senator Miller of California, and Mr. Kasson of Iowa (formerly our Minister to Austria) for an inter-oceanic canal at Nicaragua under control of the United States Government. This bill was bitterly opposed by the Panama Canal Company, by Captain Eads with his " ship railroad " scheme, and by the overland railways. Meanwhile the Administration of President Arthur was secretly negotiating a canal treaty with Nicaragua for construction on Government account, with a joint sovereignty over the Canal line and the right of fortifying terminals. The so called Zavala-Frelinghuysen treaty was ratified by the Nicaraguan Senate, but was withdrawn by President Cleveland from the United States Senate, the reasons assigned being a fear of foreign complications and the departure from precedents in legislation. Had this treaty been ratified the Canal would have been completed in 1887. The friends of the enterprise were not disheartened, but their attempt to construct with American private capital were frustrated mainly by the failure of the Marine Bank of New York, which also ruined General Grant financially.

But the demand for an inter-oceanic canal was steadily increasing, as it has subsequently increased, until it has become a national demand, recognized by both great political parties, and the facility of construction at Nicaragua had been demonstrated by repeated surveys with instruments of precision. But this concession lapsed, and in 1886 was formed the " *Nicaragua Canal Association* " and a new concession was obtained from Nicaragua and Costa Rica, a payment of $100,000 gold being made as an evidence of good faith. Surveying was resumed in 1887 under the auspices of the new association, for the purpose of developing every possible improvement in location, and borings of the canal excavations to its bottom, were made at every thousand feet. The labors of this survey may be illustrated by the fact that, although the canal in excavation is only 26⅞ miles, not less than 4000 miles of survey were made, including cross sections, embankments locks, construction railways, breakwaters, etc.

The *Nicaragua Canal Construction Company* was incorporated September 21st, 1887, under the Presidency of Francis A. Stout, Esq., subsequently succeeded by A. C. Cheney, Esq., and by Hon. Warner Miller. *The Maritime Canal Company of Nicaragua* was incorporated by act of the Congress of the United States, approved February 20th, 1889, by President Cleveland. Hon. Hiram Hitchcock and Thomas B. Atkins Esq., have been respectively, President and Secretary of this Company since its organization. This Company made a contract with the Construction Company for construction, and the work was proceeded with until the world wide financial panic of 1893, when the Construction Company suspended, and its affairs having been liquidated by a Receiver, the contract for construction has been awarded to " *The Nicaragua Company,*" of which John R. Bartlett Esq. is President. Since the present concession from Nicaragua and Costa Rica, bills for construction with the aid of the Government of the United States have been introduced in the 51st and 52d Congress, but neither came to a vote. At the second session of the 53d Congress, under President Cleveland, a bill was introduced, which, with slight amendments passed the Senate and on January 25th, 1895, by a vote of 31 to 21 it was sent to the House for concurrence, without favorable result. The introduction of these bills was not obtained by the promoters of the Canal, but originated in the Senate Committee, as stated in its report. Meanwhile Congress has authorized the appointment of a technical commission of Civil Engineers to again examine the Canal line and to make a report to the President. This Commission has completed its examination and has recently returned to the United States.

Turning from this tedious history of delays procured largely by interests adverse to the public welfare, a brief description of the Canal, on which four and a half millions have been already expended, is in order.

Description.

The Nicaragua Canal may be briefly described as a summit level of navigation in fresh water, 153¼ miles long, 110 feet above the sea level, reaching within 3½ miles of the Pacific and 12¾ miles of the Atlantic Ocean. The total length of navigation is 169½ miles; there will three lift locks at each end of the summit

WHARF AT SAN JORGE, NEAR RIVAS, LAKE NICARAGUA—OMETEPE ISLAND IN THE DISTANCE.

level. It may be properly divided into four divisions ; *the Eastern; the San Francisco; the River and Lake,* **and** *the Western.*

The Eastern division from the Atlantic to the San Francisco basin, 18⅞ miles, contains three Eastern locks. Three miles beyond the upper lock is the heaviest cut on the work, 2⁹/₁₀ miles long, through rock averaging 141 feet to canal bottom, and requiring four years work if daylight alone be used. This practically measures the period necessary to complete the canal, as the work at all other points can be completed in less time and simultaneously. It is probable that by the use of electric lighting, the work on the Canal can be greatly expedited, but under ordinary conditions it has been conservatively estimated as needing five years for completion by ten hours per day labor, allowing for delays. The rock from the Eastern divide above alluded to, is to be utilized in the break water at San Juan del Norte (Greytown); at the Ochoa dam and to line the embankments in the San Francisco division, which extends from the divide to Ochoa, 12½ miles. This division utilizes the depressions of four small streams, which are used for canal purposes by the construction of retaining embankments, thus saving excavation, and creating a navigable channel much wider and deeper than the excavated canal. At the western end of this division we come to the Ochoa dam across the River San Juan, 1900 feet long and 70 feet high, (maximum) raising the surface of the river 56 feet, or, to the lake level, less four feet, which allows about three quarters of an inch per mile for a slow current from the lake over the dam, probably about three quarters of a mile per hour.

Lake and River Division, 121.04 miles. The River San Juan discharges about 20,000 cubic feet water per second. It is a river of clear, fresh water 200 to 400 yards wide—a larger stream than the Sacramento in ordinary stages, but unlike it in never being flooded by excessive high water, the lake regulating its flow of water. by the Ochoa dam, slack water navigation is obtained to the lake with 4½ feet excavation for the 24 miles nearest the lake. The width of this inundated river navigation will vary with the conformation of the land, from the present width to half a mile or more. Some of the bends must be cut off to give a radius easy of navigation for the largest ships. There will be ample space in nearly all this division for ships to pass each other safely at a speed of eight miles per hour, while in the lake full speed can be maintained. Dredging in soft mud or silt deposit will be necessary at the Eastern end of the lake for 14 miles, averaging about 10 feet. The lake navigation is 56½ miles. Dredging will be necessary for 1400 feet at its western shore.

Western Division—Lake to Pacific Ocean 17.04 miles. Of this distance 11½ miles will be in excavation and 5.54 miles in the Tola Basin, a depression of 4000 acres which is flooded 30 to 70 ft. by a retaining dam 70 ft. high and 1800 ft. long. The use of depressions on the canal line is only possible on a surface canal, and has been made use of to great advantage by the engineers on the Nicaragua surveys.

The Port of Brito on the Pacific has to be created, but this can be done without risk and at moderate cost. It somewhat resembles Port Harford on the California Coast, except that the landing is on low ground, easily excavated. A breakwater 900 feet long will be extended from the headland and a shorter from and perpendicular to the beach enclosing a harbor of about 100 acres, which, with the enlarged prism of the canal contiguous thereto, will create all the harbor needed, especially as the splendid harbor in the Tola basin will be only 3½ miles distant, and being fresh water will be generally preferred. I may here remark that this advantage *of a fresh water canal* cannot be overestimated, both in the cleaning of animal and vegetable growths on the bottoms of iron and steel ships; in the abundant supply for boilers and general use, and in the prevention of damage by the toredo-navalis and limnoria, which so rapidly destroy timber, especially in tropical sea water.

The Port of San Juan del Norte (or Greytown) at the Atlantic terminus was a fine harbor thirty-five years ago, but has been damaged by silt deposit from the Rio San Juan, and by drifting sands of the ocean beach. The plans for the restoration of this harbor involves a cost of $2,550,667. A breakwater about 3000 feet long has to be constructed to protect the entrance from the drifting sands outside, and the channel to leeward thereof dredged to a depth of 30 feet minimum. About 1000 feet of this jetty has been already constructed, and the success which has attended the work thus far gives assurance of the ultimate results anticipated when the seaward end reaches the 6½ fathom curve. The restoration of this harbor was the most difficult problem of the Canal, there being nothing else in the work difficult of execution, the problem being merely one of finances.

The Port of San Juan del Norte is often miscalled Greytown, a name distasteful to Nicaraguans, having been first used when the British Government seized the Port and placed there Sir George Grey as military Governor. The eastern seaboard of Nicaragua was evacuated by Great Britain on the ratification of the Clayton-Bulwer Treaty, which our Government contends is now practically discarded, having been repeatedly violated by Great Britain; but it has never been formally abrogated.

The capacity of the Canal will be 20,440,000 tons which can be doubled by duplicating the locks. The Suez Canal has passed in 1894 8,059,106 tons, although this was considerably exceeded in 1891.

The amount received from tolls in 1894 was $14,770,081; receipts from passengers not stated; rate of toll averaged exactly $1.83 per ton. The Nicaragua Canal will open in 1900 with an assured tonnage of 8,730,000 tons, which will rapidly increase. The time of passing through the Canal is placed at twenty-eight hours for steamers or sailing vessels in tow, including lockages.

The fact that the Nicaragua Canal has the great advantage of being operated with fresh water has already been alluded to. The destructive work of the "teredo navalis" and of the "limnoria" will be unknown, and all wooden structures under water will become comparatively permanent improvements, whereas in tropical sea water their life would not be over two to three years. Of greater importance still is the advantage to iron shipping. The rapidity with which the bottoms of iron and steel ships foul in sea water is well known. Indeed, since we have commenced the construction of an iron and steel navy, the question of docking has become one of importance and expense. An iron ship should be docked every six months if her bottom is to be kept in good order; otherwise not only is more fuel consumed and her speed greatly retarded, but the bottom plates become "pitted" and if too long foul, ruined. It is a well known fact that marine growths on a ship's bottom when taken into fresh water at once die, and when the ship moves drop off. The inner harbors of the Canal and the Lake will become favorite stations for the cleaning of ships' bottoms and a saving can thereby be made in the expense of docking often equal to the tolls charged for the use of the Canal. It will also be no small advantage that naval vessels awaiting orders on the Canal will always be prepared for sea duty with clean bottoms and boilers full of fresh water.

The cost of the Canal has been very carefully estimated by Engineer Menocal, and by two Boards of Consulting Engineers, one in the United States and one in England. Menocal makes a cost of $65,084,176 exclusive of bankers' commissions, discounts on securities and interest during construction. The English Board exceeded this by six hundred thousand dollars, a remarkable concurrence. The American Board of Supervising Engineers out of an abundant caution took Menocal's estimates, and where they were found higher than their own retained them, but rejecting them when lower than their own, and substituting their own figures. In this way they raised the cost to $87,799,570, and conclude their report with the statement that the enterprise is full of promise. All these estimates include a 25 per cent. contingency. As a commercial problem I have always preferred to anticipate necessary a cost of $100,000,000, which will make the Canal fully as profitable as Suez, which is the best large investment in the world.

That great work the *Chicago Drainage and Ship Canal* which will unite Chicago to the Mississippi at Alton, is being built at a cost very much less than the Nicaragua estimates. The improvements made since Menocal's estimates of 1872, in excavating machinery are very striking. I append a comparison of his prices for work compared with the prices now being paid at Chicago:

NICARAGUA ESTIMATES—1872.		CHICAGO DRAINAGE CANAL.—1895.	
Per cubic yard.		Per cubic yard.	
Dredging	20 to 30 cts.		
Earth excavation	40 to 50 cts.	Dredging	5½ to 8 cts.
Rock "	$1.25 to $1.50	Earth excavation on bank	19 cts.
Rock subaqueous	$5.00	Rock "	74 cts.
Embankments, earth from cuts	20 to 30 cts.	" " minimum	59 cts.
" rock from cuts	40 to 50 cts.	Earth excavation carried away as far as ne-	
" earth from cuts	.70 cts.	cessary av	30 cts.
" rock from cuts	$1.50	Rock, subaqueous	$1.75
Masonry concrete and stone	$6 to $10		

The Chicago Drainage Canal has forty miles in excavation, and one hundred and twenty-one feet lockage elevation. The Nicaragua Canal has twenty-six and three-quarter miles in excavation and one hundred and ten feet lockage elevation. The remarkable decrease in the cost of Chicago work shows the advance in the science of Canal excavation by machinery in 25 years, and is a happy augury for the Nicaragua Canal, although there must be less difference than above indicated, for at Chicago every convenience is at hand for cheap work whereas these conveniences must be exported to Nicaragua. But it proves conclusively that the cost of the Nicaragua Canal should not exceed the estimates, and may be less than Menocal's figures.

The splendid profession of the Civil Engineer finds in the Nicaragua Canal a source of gratification and delight. I have conversed with very many practical men who have passed over the route, and when they have been shown the skill with which the project has been developed, the laborious surveys made, the borings of canal prism to its bottom and other details, their admiration has been unbounded. As remarked by Senator Morgan of Alabama, "the most fervid imagination is surprised and captured by this splendid reality." The reader will find pleasure in comparing the length and altitude of the instrumental surveys made by the United States Government across the various American inter-oceanic routes.

RANCH HOUSE NEAR CANAL LINE. COCOA PALM AND BREAD FRUIT TREE.

	Name.	Length miles.	Altitude feet.
1.	Tehuantepec	150	755
2.	Nicaragua	169	152
3.	Panama	42	295
4.	San Blas	30	1145
5.	Caledonia-Tuyra	87	1008
6.	Atrate-Tuyra	115	800
7.	Atrate-Truando	125	950
8.	Atrate-Napipi	180	778

Reconnaisance surveys were made at three other routes on the Darien Isthmus. It will be noted that Nicaragua has by far the lowest elevation and is the only fresh water canal. The San Blas route is the shortest between the oceans; in fact the tide waters of the Pacific and Atlantic there approach each other within twenty-three miles, but a mountain barrier stands in the way, with a very bad climate to aid it in forbidding canalazation at that point.

The cross section of the Nicaragua Canal is 5712 square feet against 3700 square feet at Suez:

The locks are now arranged for a length of 650 feet, depth 30 feet, width 80 feet. The lifts are as follows :

Lock No. 1, Eastern Division, 31 feet ; Lock No. 4, Western Division, 42.5 feet ; Lock No. 2, Eastern Division, 30 feet ; Lock No. 5, Western Division, 42.5 feet ; Lock No. 3, Eastern Division, 45 feet ; Lock No. 6, Western Division, variable.

Lock No. 6, Western Division, has a variable lift, owing to the rise and fall of tide at the Pacific terminus of the Canal, but averages 25 feet lift, the lake level being maintained at 110 feet. The apparent discrepancy in lift of locks on Atlantic and Pacific Division is caused by the allowance for regulated flow of the San Juan River from the Lake to the Ochoa dam. *Forty-five minutes* are allowed for each lockage, the experience at the Sault St. Marie Canal having proven this sufficient. *The supply of lockage water* is, under the utmost capacity of the Canal, over ten times the demand that can be made upon it—the magnificent inland sea of Nicaragua draining a water shed of over 8000 square miles, with an average rain fall of 55 inches per annum, and its area of 1,400 square miles, completely regulating the outflow through the outlet to the Atlantic—the San Juan River. A guard gate will be placed on the Western Division near the Lake, which can be closed when necessary to empty the locks near the Pacific, and a similar gate may be needed above the locks on Eastern Division.

In the study of this question there is at first a preference for a *sea level* canal over a *lock canal*, and indeed were it possible to imitate nature and thus construct a passage way at the American Isthmus, at a cost or within the time that is within comprehension, it would be preferable. At Suez it was feasible because of the simplicity of the conditions—a cut through the sand, with a summit 85 feet above sea level, and practically without a rainfall. But, at the American Isthmus the important question of *drainage* has to be considered as a controlling factor, the rainfall being heavy. A sea level canal is necessarily *the drainage ditch of the entire vicinage*, while a lock, surface canal, *does not disturb* in an appreciable degree *the natural drainage* of the surrounding territory. At the Panama Isthmus it has proven, as was foreseen by the United States Government Engineers, an *insurmountable obstacle*, and, while the rainfall there is very heavy at times, 260 inches annually at Colon and about 85 inches at the city of Panama and with the Chagres River flood waters an unmanageable factor, it is a question if the necessary lockage water can be provided. There is, in fact, far too much water, but it is unmanageable.

It is the unique existence of that magnificent inland sea at Nicaragua, that solves this question—*an abundance of water under control, at all times*. Without it no American Isthmus Canal would be possible, unless by a lock Canal at Panama under disadvantageous conditions or by tunneling one of the Darien routes, and for a ship canal tunneling has been condemned by all engineers, as being unsafe and in every way unacceptable to the commercial world that will pay for the use of the Canal.

As above stated, it is *the great lake*, and its *outlet to the Atlantic*, with *the low summit level* that makes the Nicaragua Canal a commercial possibility. How much nature has there done to aid the Engineer is proven by the fact that *in the natural condition, a six hundred ton steamer can leave the Atlantic and approach within 12½ miles of the Pacific!* Is it surprising that, for ages the Nicaragua route has been considered the Gateway between the Oceans, and that the great nations look upon it with envious eyes? It is recognized *as one of the keys of the World's commerce* and *a military position of unique importance*. The mind of the investigator is entranced with the splendid reality. Nature invites the capitalist and civil engineer to fully solve the great problem by the partial solution already offered.

THE NICARAGUA CANAL.

Its National Importance.

The political conditions connected with the inter-oceanic canal have been very fully discussed by the United States Senate in executive session, and occasionally a fairly informed editorial writer has published his opinions thereon, but the general public has very little idea of the subject. When President Monroe in December 1823 enunciated the great national principle now bearing his name as the "Monroe Doctrine," he referred to military and naval projects by the European Powers forming the "Holy Alliance." It was well understood then that European Powers intended an aggressive policy against the infant American Republics. There was a stalwart Americanism in those days and patriotism was not considered a vulgarity by Anglomaniacs on the Atlantic seaboard. Our Government informed European Powers that "*we could not view any interposition for the purpose of controlling, in any manner, the destinies of independent American powers, in any other light than as a manifestation of an unfriendly disposition toward the United States.*" The language is plain enough, and the sentiment of the American people on this question is well understood. It took a practical shape when Sheridan, at the conclusion of our civil war, was ordered to the Rio Grande with 100,000 veteran troops, and Louis Napoleon diplomatically notified that it would be agreeable to us to have him withdraw his French troops from Mexico, in which reasonable request he acquiesced. This practical application of the Monroe Doctrine was a necessity to our national safety and a precedent which established it. It has proven the falsity of the assertion that the Monroe Doctrine is an *intangible theory* in our foreign policy, *the world knows what it means*, but aggressive powers, wanting more territory, will occasionally try our self respect and our patriotism by the application of test cases, always prepared to recede if we are firm in our application of the famous national policy, born from the necessities of our position when the nation was comparatively weak, but full of sterling patriotism.

What reason have European powers to complain of our policy in this respect? If we assume that it is our national duty to control the Nicaragua Canal, is not our position as reasonable as the control of the Suez Canal by Great Britain? Would that power submit to our interference in the management of the Suez Canal or in its political and military control? If that is her highway to India, the Nicaragua Canal is our highway between integral portions of our country, and, in fact, as well expressed by President Hayes, "*a part of our coast line.*" In 1884 President Arthur and Secretary of State Frelinghuysen negotiated the Zavala-Frelinghuysen Treaty with Nicaragua, giving our Government the right of joint sovereignty over two and a half miles on each side of the Canal, with the right to fortify the terminals—in fact, permitting us to build and own the work jointly with Nicaragua, binding us to its military protection. This treaty was withdrawn from our Senate by the successor of Mr. Arthur, the present Chief Executive, for reasons which were entitled to respect, and this necessitated construction by a company formed for the purpose, and possessed of concessions from Nicaragua and Costa Rica, the rights of navigation of a part of the

NATIVE HOUSES NEAR SAN JUAN RIVER—CAMP OF U. S. SURVEYING CORPS.

Rio San Juan entitling the latter Republic to an interest in the Canal. Personally I much regret that the Canal was not completed under the Zavala-Frelinghuysen treaty, but fully appreciating President Cleveland's reasons, I can see how through the intervention of a Company, the great desideratum of *government control* can be attained by such a use of the national credit as will secure this to the Government, and avoid the objectionable features of the Treaty.

The Nicaragua Canal will be the great highway of our increasing commerce between the Atlantic and Pacific Coasts, and no American statesman has ever admitted the possibility of permitting the control of our isthmus transit to any European powers remanding our Navy and American commerce to the 15,000 miles voyage around the Cape, at the option of the nation controlling the Canal. Lake Nicaragua occupies a position unique in its importance to American interests. Gibraltar, or the Dardanelles cannot compare with it in the value of its military position. Upon its bosom naval fleets may float in fresh water, with clean bottoms, in a delightful climate, surrounded by a territory producing supplies for fleets and armies. Connected by telegraphic cable with Washington, such a fleet will be effective in a few days at Samoa and the Hawaiian Islands and on the Pacific Coast of America, and at Jamaica, Hayti, Cuba, the Windward Islands and the Spanish Main on the Atlantic. The Secretary of the Navy has stated in his report to the Government that it "*will double the effective force of the United States Navy.*" This alone would pay for the Canal as a national necessity.

In the eventualities which may be near at hand in Eastern Asia we cannot afford longer play "the dog in the manger" with so important a work.

Nicaragua is a sparsely settled country, with great but undeveloped resources, a healthful climate, and internal waterways insuring cheap transportation.   It will become the theater of great industrial and commercial activity, on the highway of the World's commerce.   The nation that supplies the funds to build the Canal will mostly control its policy and commerce.   The expenditure of the large sums needed for construction, the employment of skilled labor largely from the nation supplying the money, and of all available native labor as well, and the resultant influences which always accompany capital, are sufficient reasons for the national control alluded to.

As a result of construction as a private enterprise and with foreign capital, we have the incontestable right of foreign military protection to foreign property, and still, our national policy is so adverse to such protection, that its enforcement at the Canal would be almost equivalent to a declaration of war.   At the Panama Isthmus we have repeatedly landed United States forces to protect the Panama Railroad.   In fact, during the first administration of Mr. Cleveland an expeditionary force of United States Marines was sent to occupy the Isthmus until peace and protection to life and property were assured.   It was very creditably ordered and managed, fulfilling our treaty obligation with Colombia and our duty to the world.   If we do not control the Canal by *construction*, we must either subsequently *buy* or *fight* for it with the alternative of "*taking a back seat*" among the nations of the world !

The political history of the Suez Canal should be very instructive to Americans. De Lesseps had less excavation than political obstruction, for Great Britain endeavored to prevent its completion by every possible means.   But, whatever the demerits of the Great Frenchman, no one will deny his diplomatic ability and his persistency.   These characteristics, with the aid of the Khedive and of the Third Napoleon, finally triumphed over all obstacles.   When the new route to India had been opened it became a necessity to Great Britain, and Disraeli secretly bought its control for his Country.   It was the masterstroke of that great statesman; the most brilliant move he ever made, and will always endear his memory to the English heart.   When it became the military policy of Great Britain to close the Suez Canal, her ironclads filled the waterway and locked it to the navigation of the world.   No one now expects that England will abandon the vantage ground obtained in Lower Egypt and the control of her latest route to India ; never, unless under the stress of a military force which must conquer the greatest naval power of the world.   As well abandon Gibraltar, Aden Malta or Esquimault: British troops are there to stay, notwithstanding French protests !

With this history before our people, *have we not a national duty to perform in the securing of control at Nicaragua?*   If we neglect this manifest duty can we justly blame England if she secures her own interests, to our detriment?   If our great competitor for the world's commerce considers that military conditions permit her occupying and closing the Suez Canal, why not the Nicaragua Canal?   In one case she had France, a far more important military power than the United States, as an objector ; in the other case she might have the Great Republic—great in resources, but weak in its military power, except to resist invasion.   Diplomatic objections are not of much value against rifled ordnance, and there is *no greater lie* than the old assertion that "*the pen* is *mightier than the sword*," since nations are always preparing to put away the quill and draw the weapon, especially the leading European Powers!

The Pacific North West Coast has a much milder climate than the North East Atlantic littoral. The warm waters of the great Japan current—"*the Kuro Siwo*"— wash its shores in high northern latitudes and flow southerly near the Coast line to the tropics. That brilliant statesman, William H. Seward, with a prescience which immortalizes his name, knew the value of Alaska, when he bought it from Russia, and he realized that the Pacific Ocean is to be "*the scene of man's greatest achievements.*" It needs the Canal to inaugurate this brilliant future, when Alaska with her great wealth of mines, timber and fisheries shall develop her importance to the world.

Further south and nearer the Nicaragua Canal we find more population and commerce, but the same necessity for a cheap waterway to the Atlantic. The great States of Washington and Oregon, with their immense resources, halt in their onward march, and suffer an arrested development, which no railways can terminate. Their fields and forests, their fisheries and mines, are boundless sources of wealth, comparatively dormant, and awaiting the magic result of cheap water transportation by a short route to the Atlantic Ocean. *Isolation is the curse of our commercial position*, and we appeal to our countrymen in the older sections of the Republic to aid us in the solution of the question by the enactment of such legislation as will secure the Nicaragua Canal under the control of our Government and for the benefit of its people.

The Pacific Coast appeals to the patriotism of all Americans! By journeys over trackless plains, and around the Cape of Storms, our Pioneers opened the way and laid the foundation for our Pacific Empire. Before they all go over to the silent majority *they ask that our Eastern friends will aid them*, and at the same time benefit our whole country and the commercial world, by securing the speedy construction of the Nicaragua Canal.

To our legislators in Congress we can urge the Canal on the broad ground of the *national welfare* and *national prestige*. We ask them to discard party prejudice and the fear of a want of precedent : *the conditions are unique and the duty plain.* To such of our countrymen as fear the Canal in competition with other transportation interests, we respectfully beg a fair consideration of the question in a liberal sense, and a careful reading of the subsequent article "*The Nicaragua Canal and the Railroads.*" The Canal, we are fully confident, will injure no vested interest, and should receive their good will and active aid. And we also suggest to them that they are powerless to prevent its construction—at most they can only succeed in placing a foreign control over our coast line waterway, to the detriment of our country, by opposing "*an American Canal under American control.*"

The Problem of Cheap Transportation.

The question of cheap transportation is at this time attracting more attention than any other subject connected with the future of the Pacific Coast ; and this may well be the case since upon the cheap carriage of the products of our soil and industry to the world's markets depends, very largely, the prosperity of our people. Railways have accomplished wonders in this direction, considering what was expected of them in years gone by ; but this method of transportation has its limitations even where competition exists.

In the economy of modern civilization railways perform an important and necessary function. In the transportation of passengers, mails, specie, and perishable property they are indispensable. In a continental country like ours they have become an absolute necessity to our national life in time of peace, and equally so, as a means of defense, in time of war. It has been remarked that no railroad manager knows at how low a figure freight can be carried by steam and rail until he tries it ; of course he would not be foolish enough to try it unless it became necessary to do so. The Pacific Coast has important waterways which are competent to provide for a great part of her internal transportation, but selfish influences and public apathy have permitted these natural highways to become almost worthless in many instances.

When the writer arrived at San Francisco in June 1850, the vessel which brought him around Cape Horn went to Sacramento City to discharge, sailing up the river, the water of which was then so clear that fish could be seen swimming in it. Now, flat-bottom, stern wheel steamers make their way there with difficulty in the dry season and it has become a muddy stream. The duty of deepening and improving these internal waterways rests upon the Government of the Republic ; and our people should persistently work to secure appropriations for this purpose, and then see that they are judiciously expended. Wherever there is interior water-transportation freights are low, every one who has freight to transport knows this, and our transportation laws recognize it.

One of the most striking instances of the effect of cheap water-transportation is found at the St. Mary's Canal, between Lakes Superior and Huron. In the subsequent paper herewith presented, "*The Nicaragua Canal and the Railroads*," the work of this waterway, its enormous capacity and economy, are fully explained. It is passing 25 per cent. more freight annually than the Suez Canal, and is indispensable to the prosperity of that section of the country. Railways have there been found incompetent to deal alone with the problem of cost which controlled the question of its development and prosperity.

Leaving the question of internal transportation, we proceed to consider the question of ocean carriage where it competes with railways. The following statement of comparative cost was furnished me by the late William J. McAlpine, an eminent civil engineer and an unquestioned authority on the subject:

COST OF TRANSPORTATION PER TON PER MILE, EXCLUSIVE OF CAPITAL INVESTED.

1. Ocean voyages by sail or modern freight steamers.................................	1	mill
2. Shorter, or voyages of medium length..	1¼	"
3. Short coasting voyages..	2	"
4. Canals (excluding ship canals)...	4	"
Each lock is equal to one additional mile.		
5. Smaller canals with greater lockage...	6	"
6. Railways with favoring grades, loads in direction of descending grades, in excess of loads ascending..	8	"
7. Railways, heavy grades and unfavorable tonnage movement preponderating in one direction...	15	"
8. Railways of usual grades, and average freight movement each way.................	10	"

COLONEL SENOR DON EVARISTO CARAZO (DECEASED).
The President of Nicaragua who signed the Canal Concession.

As an illustration of number six: On the Reading Coal Railroad a locomotive exerts the same power to haul a train of one hundred loaded cars to market that it does to haul back the empty cars, but this is presented as a somewhat exceptional case.

Since the above table was formulated, the increase in size of ocean steamships, the adoption of triple and quadruple expansion engines for ocean service, and other improvements therewith, have still further increased the disparity between the cost of transportation by land and sea. There has also been improvement in the manufacture of locomotives, but not to the extent developed in the latest marine engines.

It must be remembered, also, that the differences herein noted are *exclusive of interest on capital*, and, when this enormous difference is considered, the ocean being a free highway, and, as a general thing, all waterways comparatively so, it will be apparent how impossible it is for the most favorably located railways to compete with water transportation.

The modern improvements in marine engines applied to large iron steamships enable them to compete with vessels propelled by sail alone, especially on short voyages, under ordinary conditions, the steamship being able to make at moderate speed about three to three and a half voyages to one of the sailing vessel in the same period and over the same course. It will be noticed, consequently, that sailing ships have the best conditions for successfully competing with steam on voyages of great length—for instance around Cape Horn and the Cape of Good Hope, in various directions. This is, in fact, the last hold of sailing ships in competition with steam upon the great oceans, and even this is being successfully contested. It may be further remarked that the ocean is free to all, and the expense of improving internal waterways is borne by the people at large, through their Government.

The depth of water at the principal ports of the world has placed a limit on the size of ships, and that limit appears to have been reached. It is a striking fact that a ship drawing twenty-four feet of water is too large for three-quarters of the harbors of the world. The trans-Atlantic steamships of largest tonnage can only pass Sandy Hook and Liverpool bars at top of high tide, and the San Francisco bar has spots on it of only thirty feet depth, on which deeply laden ships have occasionally struck. It is possible that the tonnage may be still further moderately increased by changing the model, but the limit in this direction is small, as stability is a desideratum which cannot be ignored, while excessive stability must be avoided to attain an easy movement in a sea way.

The use of auxiliary steam with full sail power has never been a success in mercantile practice, and, as marine engines have been improved upon and adapted to larger ships, has been almost entirely discarded. But the use of sail power as an auxiliary can never be economically discarded. It is the cheapest motive power that can be used afloat, and while it has been fashionable of late to dispense with it for naval purposes, the fallacy of so doing is acknowledged by many naval experts. On the long voyages by steam, especially through the trade wind regions, and for naval vessels cruising in time of peace either full or auxiliary sail power is too valuable and economical to be permanently discarded, being an element of safety as well as stability and making the cruiser, if necessary, independent of fuel supply, which is not always obtainable and is always expensive.

While nature thus appears to have placed a limit on the tonnage of sea-going ships, there appears no known limit to the method or power of propulsion. In the development of electricity we may look for a motive power applicable to navigation. Electric ships appear to be a certainty in the near future, since that power has been already successfully applied to the propulsion of small vessels for interior navigation. Under any circumstances that can be foreseen, however, water transportation will continue to be the cheapest known to commerce, and in the development of maritime commerce San Francisco must make its mark in the history of modern cities. Upon its maritime commerce will always very largely depend the prosperity of the Pacific Coast. Three-fifths of the globe is covered with navigable waters, affording a basis of cheap transportation, inviting the energy and the skill of mankind. Navigation has opened the path to empire, and its development creates a brave and hardy race, ready to uphold the liberties of the nation and the honor of its flag.

As an example of the latest practice in ocean navigation by steam, the following examples of first-class passenger and freight steamships are presented.

A typical British cargo steamship, now running between New York and England, of 8,300 register tons, carries 10,000 tons dead weight when fully laden, at a round voyage expense of $26,000, or $1.30 cost per ton across the Atlantic ; 3165 knots, on an average speed of 13 knots (faster than the most economical speed, which may be placed at 9½ to 10 knots per hour). She should do better on the smooth water voyage through the Canal.

The distance from San Francisco to Brito is 2695 miles ; through the Canal 169⁴/₁₀ miles ; from San Juan del Norte, the Atlantic terminus, to New York 2060 miles. Total distance 4925 miles. Allowing 28 hours to pass the Canal, this steamship would make the trip in 16¹⁰/₂₄ days. This makes a cost of $2.02 per ton of 2240 pounds, which, with the toll now charged at Suez ($1.85 per ton), will make $3.87 per ton from San Francisco to New York. A lower Canal toll or a decreased speed, say to 10 knots, would still further reduce the cost. This steamship will carry in weight or measurement, at ship's option, as generally laden, 12,000 tons, which reduces cost to $3.53 per long ton, freight and Suez Canal toll, from San Francisco to New York in 16¹⁰/₂₄ days. The steamships " *Manitoba* " and " *Massachusetts*," of 5,673 tons gross and 3,654 tons net register, steam an average of 12½ knots on 60 tons coal per day and carry, including coal, 7,500 dead weight, with round voyage expenses of $20,000, giving nearly as good results. An English freight steamship is now being built with a measurement capacity of 17,750 tons, of which approximately 1,000 tons will be occupied for coal, leaving an enormous freight capacity, which will make her relatively much less costly to operate than the examples cited and the cheapest cargo carrier known to commerce. This ship, however, will draw when fully laden 28 feet, and, although she would pass the Canal, the navigable depth of which is to be 30 feet, a ship so large is debarred from entry into many important ports of the world.

The high-speed passenger steamships now crossing the Atlantic could make the Canal voyage from San Francisco to New York in eleven days, including time allowed for passage through the Canal. But the transatlantic round voyage expenses of these " ocean flyers " is $75,000 to $80,000, and they are not intended to carry cheaply, time being the essence of their construction.

The examples given above are authentic, and amply illustrate what the Canal can do for the producers and merchants of the Pacific Coast. It is idle to talk of land transportation on any such costs as above stated, and there are possibilities of still further decrease in cost of operating cargo steamships ; indeed, with a speed not exceeding 10 knots, these same ships can reduce the cost given above somewhat, and quite largely reduce it with a speed of 9 knots per hour. It is to be noted also that most of the cheap and bulky freight does not require high speed, cost controlling the question.

The ocean is God's great highway—nature's cheap transportation route ; an abundance of water but no watered stocks, no tracks to maintain, no switches to be left open —its use free to all on equal terms !

The discussion of this branch of the subject may be fitly terminated with a table of comparative distances, proving the saving made by the Nicaragua Canal. No other artificial waterway on the globe, now or to be constructed, can make so favorable a showing : the table is important both for study and reference.

TABLE OF DISTANCES, IN NAUTICAL MILES, BETWEEN COMMERCIAL PORTS OF THE WORLD, AND DISTANCES SAVED BY THE NICARAGUA CANAL.

Compiled from data furnished by the United States Hydrographic Office.   **Length of Sailing Routes approximate only**

Between	Around Cape Horn for Sailing Vessels.	Via Magellan for full-powered Steam Vessels.	Via Cape of Good Hope.	Via Nicaragua Canal.	Advantage over Sailing Route.	Advantage over Steam Route.
New York and San Francisco	15,660	13,174	......	4,907	10,753	8,267
" " Puget Sound	......	13,935	......	5,665	......	8,270
" " Sitka	......	14,439	......	6,177	......	8,262
" " Bering Strait	......	15,705	......	7,402	......	8,303
" " Acapulco	......	11,555	......	3,045	......	8,510
" " Mazatlan	......	12,037	......	3,675	......	8,362
" " Hong Kong	......	......	13,750	10,692	3,058	......
" " Yokohama	......	......	15,217	9,227	5,990	......
" " Melbourne	13,760	12,860	12,830	9,862	3,898	2,998
" " Auckland, N. Z.	12,600	11,599	14,069	8,462	4,138	3,137
" " Honolulu, S. Is	15,480	13,290	......	6,417	7,063	6,873
" " Callao	......	9,640	......	3,744	......	5,896
" " Guayaquil	......	10,300	......	3,227	......	7,073
" " Valparaiso	9,420	8,440	......	5,014	4,406	3,426
New Orleans and San Francisco	16,000	13,539	......	4,147	11,853	9,392
" " Acapulco	......	11,920	......	2,285	......	9,635
" " Mazatlan	......	12,402	......	2,915	......	9,487
" " Callao	......	10,005	......	2,984	......	7,021
" " Valparaiso	......	8,805	......	4,254	......	4,551
Liverpool and San Francisco	15,620	13,494	......	7,627	7,993	5,867
" " Acapulco	......	11,875	......	5,765	......	6,110
" " Mazatlan	......	12,357	......	6,395	......	5,962
" " Auckland	12,130	11,919	12,357	11,182	948	737
" " Guayaquil	......	10,620	......	5,947	......	4,673
" " Callao	......	9,960	......	6,464	......	3,496
" " Valparaiso	9,380	8,760	......	7,734	1,646	1,026
" " Honolulu	......	13,610	......	9,137	......	4,473
" " Yokohama	......	......	14,505	11,947	......	2,558

Length of Canal, in Nautical Miles	147	**Western Port of Canal** to San Francisco,	2,700
New York to Eastern Port of Canal	2,060	" " " Portland	3,345
Liverpool " " "	4,780	" " " Puget Sound	3,458
Hamburg " " "	5,127	" " " Valparaiso	2,807
Havre " " "	4,691	" " " Callao	1,537
New Orleans " " "	1,300	" " " Yokohama	7,020

THE NICARAGUA CANAL AND THE RAILROADS.

It will be conceded that the managers of the railways of the United States are among the most able and intelligent men in the Republic, indeed the most prominent among the fraternity have few equals in the world. The criticism of any policy adopted by corporations controlled by such a class of our citizens, demands a confidence born of conviction and patient inquiry. I should hardly dare attempt it but for the anecdote stating that when Westinghouse visited Commodore Vanderbilt to induce the adoption of his system of air brakes, he was met with the assertion from the veteran steamship and railroad millionaire that "*he had no time to spend with fools*!" No brighter intellect has developed in the transportation interests of our country than Cornelius Vanderbilt, although Mr. Huntington and Jay Gould may be classed as his peers. If then, so able a man could make so pronounced a mistake, I may be excused if I respectfully criticize another point in the policy of our main East and West railroad managers. I recall that the late Count De Lesseps said to me in 1880—"Captain, *great Engineers make great mistakes* and *little Engineers* make *little mistakes*," and he added with a characteristic shrugging of his shoulders, "Captain Eads is a great Engineer !" It is the weakness of humanity to err, and men of great affairs make great mistakes because they handle great interests.

That cynical philosopher Carlyle, remarks that "*the course of human action can be safely predicated upon the fact of human selfishness.*" If this be true of individuals, no less can be expected from corporate policy. But if corporate policy be proven in error, and conviction follows the argument, that policy will be changed. I can at least present such argument as appears to me conclusive, and request for it a fair consideration.

It is well known that the only active opponents of the Nicaragua Canal are the Railway systems running East and West. Legislation which would, ere this, have secured "an American canal under American control," has been prevented by their influence in Congress. The managers of these Railway systems entertain the idea that the Canal will create a competition in freights which they desire to avoid, or at least, postpone, as long as possible. Indeed, the future competition is a certainty, but I hope to demonstrate that the assured compensation far outweighs it, and that the best friends of the Canal should be the Railway managers who have so actively opposed its construction. While the cost of water transportation compares with that by land in the ratio of from one to five to one to ten, in accordance with the conditions of each case, water transportation has its restrictions, and cannot divert from the competing railway, passenger or freight business demanding quick transit, while it is a wonderful developer of that class of transportation, as I shall endeavor to prove. Bauci

A most conclusive instance of this is the history of the development of the Lake Superior region in connection with the Sault St. Marie Canal, uniting the great Lakes. When that Canal was opened, the railroad companies in the vicinity feared a serious diversion of their carrying trade. The result was exactly the opposite. The cheap freights by water through the canal rapidly developed the surrounding region, population increased, mines were opened, new farms cultivated, new towns founded, and the railway

WILLIAM L. MERRY,
Consul General, Republic of Nicaragua, to the Western States and Territories
of the United States.

facilities proved so inadequate to the development that they have been duplicated, and
in some instances quadrupled. Development of this character means a great increase
of population, and the carriage of passengers pays a railroad far better than freight. I
may truthfully state that millions of tons of ores that have passed through the Sault St.
Marie Canal for Cleveland and other points south, for reduction, would now be lying
in their native ore beds but for the cheap water transportation which permitted their
profitable handling. So rapidly has this water-borne commerce augmented that in 1894,
during the period that the St. Mary's Canal was free of ice, a greater tonnage passed
through it than through the Suez Canal, making it to-day the World's greatest artificial
waterway! As a matter of fact, the railway companies could have better afforded to

have built the canal than to have remained without its aid in the development of their tributary territory ! Incidentally I may also state that this canal is a standing proof of the ability of locks to handle an enormous tonnage with economy. The immense tonnage passes through the St. Mary's Canal locks by day and at night, with the aid of electric lights, practically without accident or delay, and the pressure for transit has so increased that the United States Government is now constructing a new lock to accommodate shipping which will be opened in 1896, making the second large lock to be operated in overcoming the same difference in level.

Returning to the main question before us, we have the Erie Canal, which, although free to navigation, has so aided the development of the territory tributary to the railways running parallel thereto, that we now have a double track road on each side, crowded with traffic !

These two instances would appear to be conclusive, but they could be multiplied in less conspicuous instances did space permit.

The history of the Southern Pacific Company illustrates the cheapness of water transportation in another way. Although controlling a railway line across the Continent, the very able gentleman at the head of this great corporation bought out the Morgan Steamship Company, operating between his gulf terminus at New Orleans and New York, under exceptional disadvantages of ocean navigation, through the Florida Stream. By its aid he has practically dictated the traffic policy of all the transcontinental railways except the subsidized Canadian Pacific Railway, and even this latter cannot at times, safely disregard his demands ! So far as I can ascertain, no railroad manager claims that the Morgan Steamship Line injures the traffic of the railways between New Orleans and New York ; on the contrary, it supplements their usefulness.

That the Nicaragua Canal will divert heavy freight from the overland railways we may be assured ; otherwise it would little benefit our people to decrease the ocean carriage to the markets of Europe and our Eastern seacoast nearly ten thousand miles. It is in the rapid development of the entire Pacific Coast that the compensation would result. The Pacific Coast of the United States is now isolated from the markets for our products. It cannot be expected that over two mountain chains and over three thousand miles the locomotives can compete with the five thousand ton steamer that carries in one cargo the load of 333 cars of 30,000 pounds each. The products of our Coast are mostly bulky and relatively cheap ; they must have very low freight to enable them to compete in the world's markets and leave anything to the producer. That the producers of these products have generally nothing left under the present conditions after paying freight and charges, is too well known to need proof. The Sacramento Valley which has absolutely decreased in population and in the number of landowners during the past fifteen years, is a striking proof of this, for there is no more fertile valley in the world. The small landowners could not live : they have been foreclosed or have sold out, and the land has generally reverted to larger holdings. Certainly, no condition can be more unpromising to the railways in that region. And this condition is obtaining elsewhere ; relief must come or we shall untimately have a few large landowners (the railway companies among them) and a scant population to patronize railroads or merchants.

Stagnation now rules the industrial interests of the Pacific Coast. Our lumber industry is practically at a stand still and has been unremunerative for some years. Our wheat industry is dead so far as profits in the export trade are concerned. Our fruit industry remains remunerative in exceptional cases, but before the cheap water-way to the Atlantic can be completed will arrive at the same condition. Indeed, horticulturists are complaining bitterly of high freights to Eastern markets and demanding relief. Our lands are neglected because it does not generally pay to cultivate them, our merchants find their clientage decreasing ; our manufacturers have in many instances closed up their factories and discharged their workmen.

If this be the result, after twenty-five years of direct railway connection with the East, well may our people look for a remedy in different conditions. And these conditions will certainly follow the construction of the Nicaragua Canal, without injury to our present inland transportation interests. Not only will the Canal give us a free outlet for our products, but it will open the highway for a desirable European immigration. I write *desirable* advisedly, for nothing can be so objectionable as the flooding of this country with the communists, anarchists and lazzaroni of Europe. It will cost more to come here than to go to our Eastern seaports, and we shall, it is to be presumed, receive the best grade of immigrants. But this question is not germain to the purpose of this paper and may be dismissed with the assertion that it is high time to legislate for our protection therein. It is in the advent of *an increasing population* and the *resultant industries* that the railway systems, now antagonistic to the Canal, will find their compensation for a diversion of a part of their through traffic. Their managers admit that the through haul has always been less remunerative than the short haul, and that its adjustment meets with increasing difficulties every year. New and powerful competitors are coming into the field. The subsidized Canadian Pacific, the Atchison & Santa Fe, the Northern Pacific, the Panama and Tehuantepec Isthmus, the Guatemala Northern and the Cape Horn route, will all compete for through business. Even the Suez Canal is a disturbing factor in the overland carriage of the products of China and Japan. With the completion of the Nicaragua Canal the policy of our Pacific Coast railroads will *necessarily change.* The local haul to and from tide-water will have precedence, and Pacific Coast ports will become distributing points for the products of China and Japan. Instead of competing with the Suez Canal for this trade at New York to such an extent that the trade of San Francisco in the same products is discriminated against, our railways will contest it by distribution eastward from the seaboard of the Pacific. The flow of Asiatic commerce to the Atlantic, passing San Francisco at its very doors, on the shortest ocean route, it will, with San Diego, become a port of call for transpacific steamships, their passengers and a part of their freight swelling the income of our railroads, while these same steamships will fill their vacant cargo space with Pacific Coast products, hauled to tide water by rail. Under these conditions even the railways eastward from the Missouri River will benefit more largely by the increased population and development of the Pacific Slope than can be lost by them on any diverted traffic. It is in fact an impossibility that any railway will be injured by the conditions alluded to and which will result from the completion of the Nicaragua Canal.

The Pacific Coast of the United States is in a transition state. The isolation of pioneer days has passed. We are being brought face to face with the competition of the whole world. It is our railroads that have brought us to this condition, and they cannot ignore the result. We cannot stop half way—that policy has been proven

A steamship from Yokohama to the Atlantic, via Canal, lengthens her voyage only 91 miles by calling at San Francisco, and from Hongkong to the Atlantic lengthens it only 20 miles.

ruinous. We must throw down all the barriers impeding the cheapest intercourse, and make our fight for progress on the principles of competition. This the Nicaragua Canal will do for us. The ocean is a free highway given us by an Almighty hand ; no right of way, no wear and tear, no bonded indebtedness for track and stations, no depreciation.

> " Not so Thou !
> Same as creations dawn beheld, Thou rollest now ! "

We can no longer endure the condition of isolation which has induced an arrested development. We need a greater population, small land holdings with more owners; we must have a shorter cheap water route for our lumber, our cereals and other products, which the railways cannot haul across the continent and thence ship to Europe with profit. An increase of desirable population is an absolute necessity to our prosperity. It is not the half-million in San Francisco but the millions of contented residents in our great interior that we need the most. The city of San Francisco is already larger than the population in its tributary interior warrants, and our great seaport will grow when conditions warrant ; indeed, when its wharves are crowded with the steam-

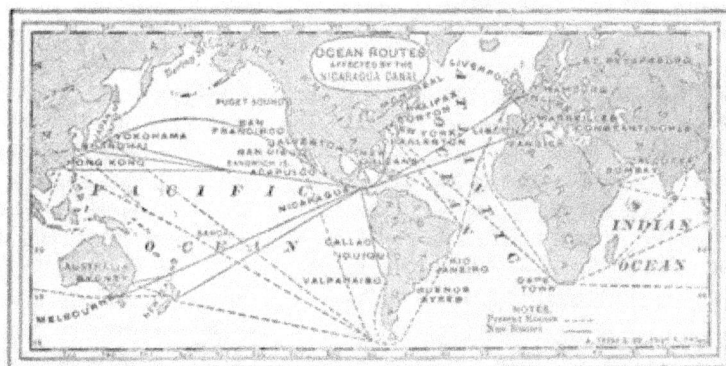

ships from Atlantic ports it will become the commercial center of the Pacific Coast— *that* it must become under any supposable conditions, for the impress of an Almighty hand rests with approval upon our unequaled position as a seaport, and upon the noble rivers and fertile valleys which are tributary to it.

Will the development which I have imperfectly delineated inflict injury upon our railway interests? How vain such a conclusion! California could better afford to pay for the Nicaragua Canal herself than be without it, and our railway systems can better afford to aid its speedy construction than to oppose it.

During the five years necessary for construction the imperative necessity for the Nicaragua Canal will have been accentuated, and when it is in active operation our railway systems will regard it as an ally in development and transportation, while our people will refer to the present period, prior to the Canal, as the arrested development which, like a black cloud hung over our beautiful Pacific Coast to be succeeded by the sunshine of such healthy progress and prosperity as we have never known ! Our country has here an empire, with products and climate so diversified that they excite the wonderful admiration of close observers. *The bane of isolation* is gradually leaving it, and when the glorious day arrives that the first American steamship floats upon the Inland Sea of Nicaragua, laden with California products, our emancipation will be complete! It will inaugurate the period of increased population and increasing railroad earnings, not only for Pacific Coast railroads but for all the iron highways reaching toward the Atlantic.

The mistaken policy which opposes the elimination of nearly half the earth's circumference from the navigable distance to the great markets of Europe and the Eastern seaboard, will have become ancient history, to which allusion will only be made as a proof of the fallacy of human judgment, even among the most able minds of the age!

It is, indeed not an easy matter to predict all the changes which will result from the opening of the great inter-oceanic highway. It requires the technical knowledge of a navigator, the commercial acumen of an experienced merchant, and the prescience of a wise statesman to forecast the result of such a change in the lines of communication between the nations of the earth, but of one thing we may be certain — the elimination of ten thousand miles of navigation from the longest ocean route on the globe cannot result otherwise than in a momentous change for the better, for time and distance are controlling factors in the prosperity of the human race, and the period of national isolation has passed.

I have not alluded to the value of the Canal to our country and to the other nations of the world, especially to the republics of the American continent. Who will deny the prestige, the political and military advantage, to the Great Republic, the development of Central American commerce by which our people will largely benefit, the increase of our mercantile marine, "the Star of Empire" marching Westward! These considerations have been apart from my main argument, and if I have convinced the reader that the Nicaragua Canal will become the ally and the complement of American railroads, instead of a competitor to be dreaded, my object will have been accomplished. So bright an intellect as William H. Seward has remarked that "the Pacific Ocean is to be the scene of man's greatest achievements." In this great history of the future our Pacific railroads will work hand in hand with the Canal, the thought of adverse interests will vanish, and a common interest in development, with increased commerce and prosperity, will supplant it. And this change of sentiment will do honor to the great minds that first admit the facts which they cannot prevent, unless they make the world move backward!

MAP OF THE WORLD, SHOWING LINES OF NAVIGATION THROUGH THE NICARAGUA CANAL.

		Knots.
The shortest practicable route from Brito to Yokohama		7,343

	Knots.	
Brito to San Francisco	2,769	
San Francisco to Yokohama	4,586	

		Knots.
Therefore the distance from Brito to Yokohama, via San Francisco, is		7,336
Therefore excess of route via San Francisco over shortest practicable route, is		93

	Knots.	
Brito to Honolulu	4,216	
Honolulu to Yokohama	3,400	

Shortest practicable route from Brito to Yokohama, via Honolulu		7,616
Therefore excess of route via Honolulu over route via San Francisco, is		324

The shortest practicable route from Brito to Hongkong		8,740

	Knots.	
Brito to San Francisco	2,769	
San Francisco to Hongkong	6,0x0	

Therefore the distance from Brito to Hongkong, via San Francisco, is		8,760
Therefore excess of route via San Francisco over shortest practicable route, is		70

	Knots.	
Brito to Honolulu	4,210	
Honolulu to Hongkong	4,917	

Therefore the distance from Brito to Hongkong, via Honolulu, is		9,157
Therefore the excess of route via Honolulu over route via San Francisco, is		367

The conditions as to the distances in Trans-Pacific Navigation apply approximately to all United States Pacific Coast Ports.

PERSONAL.

In 1858, when an officer of the United States Mail Steamship Company's steamer " *George Law*," I first visited San Juan Del Norte, the Atlantic terminus of the Nicaragua Canal. In 1862, when commanding the clipper ship " *White Falcon*," of New York, I visited its Pacific terminus, and from San Juan del Sur went to Virgin Bay, when I first beheld the magnificent inland sea of Nicaragua. The year 1863 found me at Panama, as agent for the Marshall O. Robert's Line of steamships between New York and San Francisco. I had coal-laden vessels arriving at Aspinwall (Colon), and during the year I lived at Panama went over the Panama railroad twice a week. In 1864, I took command of the steamship *America*, and remained in her two years and eight months running between San Francisco and Nicaragua. I was then appointed general agent in charge of the Nicaragua transit for the Central American Transit Company and the North American Steamship Company, of which my old and valued friend, William H. Webb of New York, was president. I practically *lived on the line of the Canal*, passing over it during nearly three years, by night and day, in steamers, boats, and canoes. The entire canal line is as familiar to me as California street. During all these years I was acquiring information in regard to the canalization of the American Isthmus. The reader may judge by the opportunities of personal investigation which I have been able to avail of, how thoroughly I have acquainted myself with the subject. So when, in the course of events, I engaged in mercantile pursuits at San Francisco, and the Canal question became a matter of public interest, I was able to take it up intelligently and with a full appreciation of its great importance to San Francisco, the Pacific Coast, to the Great Republic and to all the commercial world. Thus, while others may properly claim the initiative on the Canal question from a *political* and *military* standpoint, I can properly claim to have *first introduced the Canal question to the merchants of the United States from a commercial standpoint.* The views which were often considered visionary, are at this day universally accepted as practical, and today the Canal is the most popular enterprise before the American people. Already I see the reward of unwearied, and, on this Coast, until recently almost unaided effort, born of the conviction that the Nicaragua Canal will solve for my adopted City and State the great desideratum of cheap transportation to the markets of the world. I am so confident that I shall go from ocean to ocean over the Nicaragua Canal that I no longer permit myself to be annoyed at impediments and delays—the Canal is a certainty of the near future. There can be no more satisfactory record than thus to have made my years useful to my fellow citizens, to the Republic of Nicaragua which has honored me with its confidence, to the Great Republic, and to the commerce of the world!

WILLIAM L. MERRY.

www.ingramcontent.com/pod-product-compliance
Lightning Source LLC
Chambersburg PA
CBHW021436090426
42739CB00009B/1511

9783337319304